A Taste of culture

FOODS OF GREECE

Titles in the Series

Foods of France

Foods of Greece

Foods of Italy

Foods of Japan

Foods of Mexico

Barbara Sheen

KIDHAVEN PRESS

An imprint of Thomson Gale, a part of The Thomson Corporation

Detroit • New York • San Francisco • San Diego • New Haven, Conn. • Waterville, Maine • London • Munich

© 2006 by KidHaven Press. KidHaven Press is an imprint of The Gale Group, Inc., a division of Thomson Learning, Inc.

KidHaven™ and Thomson Learning™ are trademarks used herein under license.

For more information, contact
KidHaven Press
27500 Drake Rd.
Farmington Hills, MI 48331-3535
Or you can visit our Internet site at http://www.gale.com

LIBRARY OF CONGRESS CATALOGING-IN-PUBLICATION DATA
Sheen, Barbara. Foods of Greece / by Barbara Sheen. p. cm. — (Taste of culture) Includes bibliographical references and index. ISBN 0-7377-3033-1 (hardcover : alk. paper) 1. Cookery, Greek. 2. Greece—Social life and customs. I. Title. II. Series. TX723.5.G8S54 2005 394.1'2'09495—dc22   2005000086

Contents

Chapter 1

The Unique Flavors of Greek Cooking

Greek food is healthy and delicious. It is made with natural ingredients such as grapes, lemons, honey, nuts, tomatoes, garlic, eggplant, wild greens, beans, grains, cheese, yogurt, fresh fish, lamb, olives, and olive oil. Because different products are produced in different parts of Greece, there are regional differences in Greek menus. For example, Greek islanders and those who live in coastal areas eat more fresh fish than those who live inland. They also eat more foods that grow in warm climates, such as figs, artichokes, and almonds, than northerners do. Northern Greeks eat more cool-weather vegetables such as cabbages and leeks.

Despite regional differences, three ingredients are present in foods throughout Greece: olives, olive oil, and

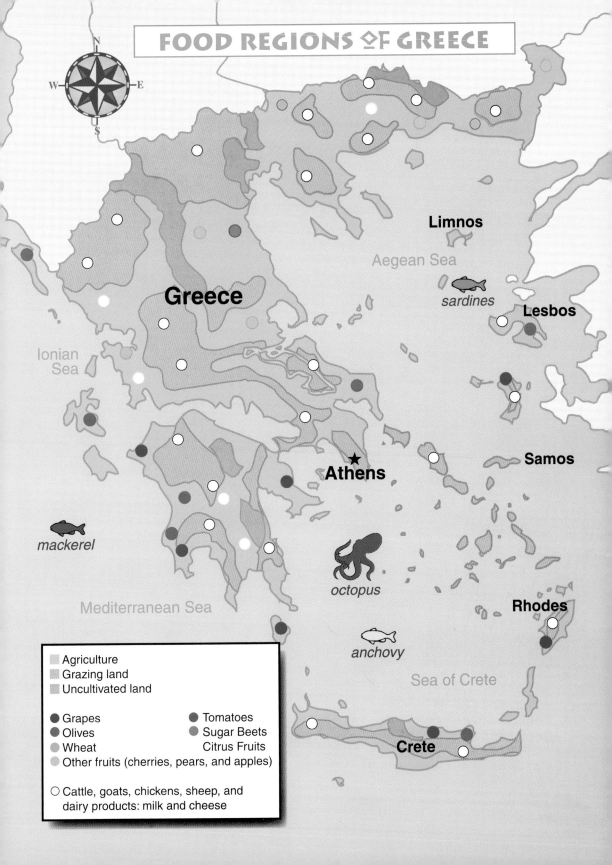

FOOD REGIONS OF GREECE

Limnos

Aegean Sea

sardines

Lesbos

Greece

Ionian
Sea

Samos

mackerel

Athens

octopus

Rhodes

anchovy

Mediterranean Sea

Sea of Crete

Crete

Agriculture
Grazing land
Uncultivated land

● Grapes   ● Tomatoes
● Olives   ● Sugar Beets
● Wheat   Citrus Fruits
● Other fruits (cherries, pears, and apples)

○ Cattle, goats, chickens, sheep, and
    dairy products: milk and cheese

A woman on the island of Crete harvests olives, a fruit that has been central to Greek life since ancient times.

lemons. These ingredients give Greek food its unique flavor.

Olives: A National Symbol

Greeks have been eating olives for eons. They have been an important part of Greek cooking and Greek life since 3000 B.C. Olives were so important to the ancient Greeks that it was a crime, punishable by death, to cut down an olive tree. Today the Greek government gives workers paid leave in November so that they can help harvest olives.

More than 100 million beautiful gray-green olive trees grow all over Greece, and a million new seedlings are planted each year. In the north, in the south, in the Greek islands—as far as the eyes can see—olive trees are everywhere.

Different Varieties

Today, Greece produces 90,000 tons (81,646 metric tons) of olives each year. One-third of the olive crop stays in Greece, where no mealtime table is complete without a bowl of olives. There are more than one hundred different varieties. There are small olives and large olives, sweet olives and bitter olives, firm olives and soft olives, green olives, brown olives, purple olives, blue olives, and black olives. Their colors change as

Wild Greens

Wild greens, or *horta* in Greek, are another important and healthy part of the Greek diet. Wild greens are edible plants that grow all over the Greek countryside. Greens such as leeks, asparagus, fennel, arugula, chard, mustard greens, and watercress are just a few of the three hundred different varieties of edible wild plants that Greeks adore.

Greeks use wild greens in salads, soups, stews, and porridges. They mix them with flour and fry them as patties. They lightly cook them in water seasoned with olive oil and lemon to make boiled salad, a favorite dish.

Greeks have been eating wild greens for centuries. Over the years, they have learned which greens are edible and tasty and which should be avoided. During World War II, when wild greens were sometimes the only food available, this knowledge kept many Greek people from starving. Today, Greeks do not have to gather wild greens for survival. Many farmers cultivate them, and vegetable markets all over Greece sell the tasty greens. Some Greek families still take weekend excursions to the country just to gather wild greens.

they ripen. All olives start out green and darken as they mature. Whether green or dark, fresh olives are bitter and tough. They must be **cured**, or preserved in salt or oil, before they can be eaten.

Each variety of olive has a unique flavor. Amphissas are soft, mild-flavored brown olives. Greek greens are firm, salty, and crunchy. The most famous olives are the slightly bitter purple kalamatas. Greeks love them all. They bake them in pies and breads such as eliopitta, a delicious crisp bread filled with whole Amphissa olives. They sprinkle them with sea salt and oil and eat them as snacks. They grind them into a tangy paste that they spread on bread. They add them to tomato sauce, which they pour over ground meat and rabbit. They combine them with dill and lemon juice to add flavor to fish and squid. No salad is complete without them. Greek chef Aglaia Kremezi explains: "The olive is basic to our lives and our identity."[1]

Olive Oil in Everything

Greeks do not just eat olives, they make oil from the little fruits too. To make olive oil, they place the olives in a metal-toothed grinder that presses out the oil. The oil that is removed during the first pressing is called **extra-virgin olive oil**. It is the finest of all olive oil. It is sweet, greenish gold, and delicious.

Each Greek consumes about 8 gallons (30 l) of extra-virgin olive oil every year. That is more than any other people on Earth. To Greeks, olive oil is more important than salt or spices. They use the oil in everything from main dishes to pastries.

Ladolemono

Greeks put this olive oil–lemon sauce over everything. They pour it over cold or hot vegetables, fish, or chicken. They baste grilled or broiled food with it or use it as a marinade. It makes an excellent salad dressing. Cooks can make more or less sauce by changing the amount of oil and lemon juice they add. It is best to use twice as much olive oil as lemon juice. Ladolemono tastes best fresh. So just make enough to use rather than storing it.

Shopping List
olive oil
lemons
parsley
scallions
oregano

Ingredients:

4 tablespoons extra-virgin olive oil
2 tablespoons fresh-squeezed lemon juice
salt and pepper to taste
Optional: you can add these spices to taste—
chopped parsley, chopped scallions, oregano

Instructions:

1. Pour the olive oil in a bowl.
2. Pour in the lemon juice. Whisk the ingredients together.
3. Add salt and pepper to taste.
4. Add one of the optional ingredients to taste.
5. Pour ingredients into a jar and shake well.

Serves 4

A Greek woman sifts through a bag of freshly picked olives. Olives help Greeks to lead long and healthy lives.

It is even used in place of butter or shortening. It gives flavor and richness to all Greek foods. Olives are marinated in it. Eggplant, garlic, and onions are fried in it. Vegetables are bathed in it. Fish and meat are rubbed with it. Salads are dressed with it. Dough is rolled in it. Sauces are made from it. Soups and stews are flavored with it. Bread is dunked in it. Even some cookies contain olive oil. Christos, a Greek man, explains: "Here oil is more plentiful than water."[2]

The Key to Long Life

Olives and olive oil are so much a part of Greek life that whenever a new baby is born, Greek families plant an olive tree. Olive trees can live for six hundred years. Although humans cannot live as long, many Greeks live to be one hundred years old. Greeks credit their longevity to olive oil.

Since ancient times, Greeks have believed that olive oil keeps them strong and healthy. Greeks are so sure that olive oil promotes good health that many Greeks eat a tablespoon of olive oil every morning, similar to the way Americans take vitamins. Scientists say that the Greeks may be correct. They say that a diet rich in olive oil protects people from heart disease. This may be why Greeks have the longest life expectancy of any people in Europe.

A Perfect Balance

Many Greeks say that another reason they live so long is because they try to balance the different elements in their lives—work and play, activity and rest. They also try to balance different elements in their cooking. That may be why Greeks love to combine lemon juice with olive oil to make a sauce or dressing they call **ladolemono**. They say the acidic sour taste of the lemon juice balances the sweet smoothness of the olive oil. Used together, they give food a unique and delicious flavor and a special aroma.

Greeks bathe salads, meats, fish, chicken, beans, and vegetables with ladolemono. They add it to mayonnaise and flavor dips and sauces with it. Greek cookbook author Diane Kochilas says: "Give a Greek a healthy portion of olive oil, a shot or two of fresh lemon juice . . . and he will gladly mix or dribble them over everything from spring lamb to roasted potatoes to a simple cabbage salad."[3]

Lemons and Eggs

Lemons are also the basis for another important Greek sauce: **avgolemono**. Creamy and tangy at the same time, avegolemono is the most popular Greek sauce. It is made by combining lemon juice, egg yolks, and chicken broth.

Greeks simmer beans and vegetables in avgolemono. They cook stuffed cabbage and grape leaves in it. They stew meat in it. They brush it on seafood. Most important, they use the sauce as the basis for soup. Avgolemono is the most beloved flavor for Greek soup. With its lemony taste and bits of egg floating on the surface, avgolemono is a nourishing and delicious base for chicken, meatball, or fish soup. It is hard to resist a fragrant steamy bowl.

Loaded with Vitamins

Greeks have been eating lemons since A.D. 700, when the first lemon tree was planted in Greece. Unlike olives, lemons are not native

A fruit market in Athens offers crates of lemons for sale.

Avgolemono Soup

Avgolemono soup is easy to make. This recipe uses canned chicken broth.

Ingredients:

3 cans chicken broth
$1/2$ cup of rice
2 eggs
juice of 1 lemon
salt and pepper to taste
Optional: chopped parsley to taste

Shopping List
chicken broth
eggs
rice
lemon

Instructions:

1. Pour the broth into a large pot and cook until it boils.
2. Add the rice, stirring until the broth boils again.
3. Lower the heat and let the soup and rice simmer for about fifteen minutes.
4. In a bowl break the eggs, add the lemon juice, and stir well.
5. Slowly drip the egg–lemon juice mixture into the soup pot, stirring constantly. The eggs will cook and look like bits of scrambled egg.
6. Add salt and pepper to taste.
7. Pour into bowls and serve hot with bread or crackers.

Serves 4 to 6 depending on the size of the bowl

The foods served in restaurants throughout Greece, like this one on the island of Santorini, are very healthy.

to Greece. They originated in Southeast Asia. Middle Eastern traders brought them to ancient Turkey. From Turkey, they soon found their way to Greece.

Greeks quickly came to love lemons, and not just for their flavor. Early Greek physicians used lemon juice to treat a number of illnesses. It was not a bad idea. Lemons are loaded with vitamin C, a nutrient that helps the body fight off germs.

Scientists say that the Greek diet, with its lemons, olives, and olive oil, may be the healthiest diet on Earth. Besides contributing to the Greek people's good health, these key ingredients have added richness, flavor, and balance to Greek cooking and Greek life for thousands of years.

Favorite Foods

Greeks combine their favorite ingredients with fresh fruit, vegetables, cheeses, poultry, meat, and fish to create hundreds of mouthwatering dishes. Among their favorites are **phyllo**, **dolmades**, **moussaka**, and **horiatiki**. Greeks adore these dishes.

Phyllo

Phyllo is a paper-thin pastry dough. The Greeks use it in hundreds of different ways. Phyllo is used to make appetizers, main dishes, and desserts. Usually, phyllo is homemade. But it takes so much effort to get it thin enough that many Greek cooks are turning to store-bought phyllo. Boxes containing twenty-five to thirty ready-made phyllo sheets are sold in pastry shops and supermarkets all over Greece.

To make phyllo, Greek cooks make a dough from flour, water, olive oil, lemon juice, and salt. They use a special long rolling pin to roll out the dough. It can take hours to roll the dough thin enough without tearing it. In addition, rolling must be done repeatedly, because phyllo is prepared in sheets. Each sheet is about 0.33 inch (0.84cm) thick and 12 by 15 inches (30 by 38cm) in size. Cooks often use dozens of sheets in just one dish. Kremezi explains: "You must be very nimble fingered and need lots of practice to be able to achieve the perfect phyllo."[4]

Sweet or Hearty Pittas

The Greeks' favorite way to use phyllo is in pittas, which are delectable dessert and main-dish pies. Greeks eat pittas day and night, for both meals and snacks, and they have been doing this for thousands of years. "Pitta," says Kochilas, "is to Greeks what pasta is to Italians—food to warm the soul."[5]

A baker on the island of Crete stretches a large sheet of phyllo dough to make it thin enough for cooking.

Spanakopitta

This spinach pie is very popular in Greece. It uses commercially prepared phyllo. Working with phyllo is difficult. Be sure to moisten it well with olive oil and follow the package directions. This recipe uses frozen chopped spinach. Creamed spinach can also be used.

Ingredients:

1/2 pound of phyllo, thawed
10-ounce package of frozen chopped spinach, thawed
1 egg
1/3 cup olive oil
1 small onion chopped
1/2 pound feta cheese, crumbled
1 teaspoon oregano
1 teaspoon black pepper

Instructions:

1. Preheat oven to 350 degrees F.
2. Place thawed spinach in a colander and drain.

Shopping List
phyllo
spinach
eggs
onions
feta cheese
oregano
olive oil

Pittas, which are served warm or cold, can be filled with almost anything. They are an excellent way for cooks to use leftovers or whatever food is on hand. Filled with honey, nuts, raisins, and sweet cheese, pittas are sugary treats. Filled with meat, cheese, and vegetables, pittas become a hearty meal. The most beloved of all pittas is spanakopitta, a spinach and cheese pitta. Other popular pitta fillings include lamb, rice, and raisins; cheese and eggs; and artichokes and tomatoes.

To make a pitta, cooks cover the bottom of a pie tin with layer upon layer of phyllo. Then they add the filling and top

3. Put a little olive oil in a pan and sauté the onions until they are a light golden brown.
4. Squeeze excess water out of the spinach, remove onions from the pan, and combine the onions and spinach in a bowl.
5. Combine feta cheese, egg, oregano, and pepper. Mix well and add to the spinach mixture.
6. Grease a 9-by-13-inch pan with olive oil.
7. Layer half of the phyllo sheets in the pan. Brush each sheet with olive oil before adding the next sheet.
8. Spread the spinach mix over the oiled phyllo sheets. Top with the remaining half of the phyllo sheets. Be sure to brush each sheet with olive oil.
9. Bake until the pie is golden brown, about forty minutes.
10. Let the pie cool before cutting and serving.

Serves 6 to 8

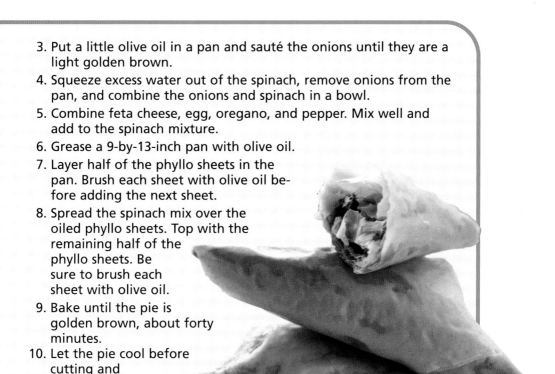

it with more layers of phyllo. Some pittas contain more than forty layers of phyllo, while others contain only two or three. The more layers, the thicker and richer the pitta.

A Perfect Wife

Pittas and phyllo are so important to Greeks that a tradition once centered around them. For example, in the past when a baby girl was born, a rolling pin was placed in her crib. It was hoped that when she grew up she would become a good phyllo maker. This would make her husband happy. Although this tradition is no longer practiced,

A woman stuffs grape leaves with rice and other tasty ingredients to make homemade dolmades.

Greek cooks know that whenever they serve pittas, happiness follows.

Dolmades

Greeks fill dolmades with some of the same fillings that they love in pittas. Another Greek favorite, dolmades are stuffed grape leaves. They are stuffed with just about anything. Rice, vegetables, and raisins are one

Fresh or Salted

Depending on the season, the grape leaves that Greek cooks use to make dolmades may be fresh or preserved in brine, like pickles. In the spring and summer, Greeks gather fresh, tender grape leaves and use them to make dolmades. In the fall and winter, when fresh leaves are not available, they use grape leaves preserved in olive oil and salt. Sold in large jars called leaf jars, these leaves are saltier and tougher then fresh leaves. In order to make them taste more like fresh leaves, cooks boil the preserved leaves before using them. This helps remove some of the salt and softens them.

A filling of lamb, rice, and mint sits on a fresh grape leaf, waiting to be wrapped into a delicious dolma.

A man on the island of Ithaca loads a basket of grapes onto his donkey. He will use the leaves to make dolmades.

popular stuffing. Lamb, mint, and rice are another. No matter what the filling, Greeks try to balance the taste by using foods with contrasting flavors, such as bitter vegetables and sweet raisins. The result is a delicious meal.

Greeks have been wrapping their food in leaves for thousands of years. The idea came from Turkey, where fig leaves were the most common wrapper. Over time Greek cooks replaced the fig leaves with grape leaves. This may have happened because grapes grow all over Greece, so the leaves have always been easy to find. And Greeks love the taste of grape leaves, which they say is sweet and tender.

Making Dolmades

To make dolmades, Greek cooks lay a moist grape leaf down flat and then place a spoonful of filling on the bottom. Then, they carefully fold the bottom and two sides of the leaf over the filling and tightly roll the leaf up to form a tube shape. Then they put the dolmades in a baking pan with a little broth and sprinkle them with ladolemono. The dolmades are cooked until the broth is absorbed and the leaves are moist and tender.

Dolmades are always served at room temperature with a slice of lemon and a spoonful of plain yogurt. Greeks eat them for lunch or supper, serve them to guests, and always take them along on picnics. Kyria, a Greek woman, explains that in her home, "it just isn't Sunday without the leaves."[6]

Moussaka

Moussaka is another favorite Greek dish. In fact, it is the national dish of Greece. Made by alternating layers of eggplant, pota-toes, onions, red peppers, and lamb under white sauce, moussaka is rich and delicious.

Horiatiki, Greek Village Salad

This delicious salad is easy to make. It uses feta cheese, which is sold in most supermarkets. Use the freshest, ripest tomatoes you can find.

Ingredients:

4 tomatoes
1 small sweet red onion
1 cup black olives
$1/3$ pound feta cheese, crumbled into small pieces
1 cucumber
1 green bell pepper
$1/4$ cup olive oil
1 teaspoon oregano
$1/2$ teaspoon garlic powder

Instructions:

1. Slice the tomatoes into six slices each.
2. Slice the onions into thin, round slices.
3. Remove the seeds from the green pepper. Cut it into round, thin slices.
4. Peel the cucumber. Cut it into thin slices.
5. Combine the cut tomatoes, onion, pepper, and cucumber in a salad bowl. Add the black olives and feta cheese.
6. Add the olive oil, oregano, and garlic powder.
7. Toss the salad and serve immediately.

Serves 4 to 6

Shopping List
tomatoes
red onion
black olives
feta cheese
cucumber
bell pepper
olive oil
oregano
garlic powder

Some people substitute zucchini for eggplant, but the basic preparation is the same. First, cooks fry the potatoes, onions, eggplant, or zucchini in olive oil. Then, they combine the meat with tomatoes and raisins and fry this mixture, too. Meanwhile, they roast the red peppers in the oven. When everything is cooked, the foods are layered in a casserole pan, covered with white sauce, and baked until the moussaka is crisp and golden brown. After it cools, it is cut into squares and served with salad and thick, crusty bread.

French Sauce

Unlike most Greek foods, the white sauce that tops moussaka contains butter rather than olive oil. Known as **bechamel** sauce, it is made with butter, milk, flour, and cheese. It comes from France. In the early 1900s, Greek chef Nikkos Tselements studied French cooking in Paris. He liked bechamel sauce so much that he used it to top moussaka. Tselements's version of moussaka became wildly popular, and soon everyone was using the sauce.

Gemistas

Dolmades are not the only stuffed food that Greeks adore. Greeks love to fill tomatoes and their favorite vegetables with many of the same fillings they use in dolmades. To do this, they hollow out tomatoes, eggplants, zucchini, and bell peppers. Fillings such as rice and ground meat or chopped eggplant, raisin, and rice are stuffed into the tomato and vegetable shells, drizzled with olive oil, and baked. Greeks call these stuffed treats gemistas. They eat them for main dishes and appetizers at lunch and supper.

Greeks at an outdoor café in Athens enjoy a meal in the twilight of a summer day.

Today people all over the world associate moussaka with Greece. Many Greeks cannot live without this mouthwatering casserole. Alexandra, a Greek teenager, explains: "The popularity of moussaka has deservedly spread. It is a delicious combination of meat, vegetables, and a thick, rich sauce. It is the most traditional Greek dish and it is absolutely delicious."[7]

Village Salad

When moussaka is served, chances are that horiatiki or village salad will accompany it. This is a favorite salad among Greeks. Horiatiki is made with fresh, juicy tomatoes, olives, onions, and crumbled feta cheese. It is then dressed with lots of olive oil. Feta cheese is a salty, white cheese made from sheep's or goat's milk. It is what makes this salad special, giving it a slightly salty flavor that Greeks adore.

Horiatiki is always served in a large family-size bowl. While everyone watches, the oldest person present pours the olive oil over the salad, tosses it, then serves it to everyone. Greeks consider this job an honor.

A Taste of Sunshine

In summer, Greeks eat horiatiki at least once a day. The salad's cool, salty flavor is refreshing. The tomatoes are likely to be fresh off the vine, brimming with juice. Greeks say that they can almost taste the sunshine.

During other times of the year, eating horiatiki reminds Greeks of summer. Kelsey, a native of Spetses, a Greek island, explains: "A well-balanced horiatiki with fresh ingredients is a delight that will bring a glow to your day even if you aren't actually sitting in the sun."[8]

No matter what the season, Greeks love eating horiatiki, dolmades, moussaka, and phyllo. The delicious flavors of these dishes delight hungry Greeks. It is no wonder that these are among their favorite foods.

3

Snacks and Sweets

Whether they are eating meaty treats or syrup-coated pastries, Greeks love to snack. They enjoy **souvlaki**, **gyros**, syrup cakes, and baklava. These are among every Greek's favorite snacks and sweets.

Greek Fast Food

When Greeks think of fast food, they think of souvlaki and gyros. Street vendors, sidewalk cafés, and neighborhood restaurants all over Greece sell these meaty treats. Busy Greeks cannot get enough of them.

In Greek, the word *gyro* means "to spin," and the word *souvlaki* means "meat on a stick." That is what these mouthwatering snacks are—meat grilled on a **rotisserie** or spinning stick. To make souvlaki and gyros, lamb seasoned

Greek men grill souvlaki, chunks of skewered lamb meat, over an open flame.

with ladolemono is placed on a long upright skewer. Then it is grilled over an open flame.

The meat cooks as the skewer turns. When the meat is crisp on the outside and juicy on the inside, the cook cuts off strips of the meat and puts them on a plate with grilled onions, tomatoes, and a piece of hot grilled bread. If the ingredients are placed inside the bread, it is called a gyro. If the bread is eaten on the side, the dish is known as souvlaki.

A spoonful of **tzatziki**, a wildly popular Greek sauce, always tops these treats. Tzatziki is a creamy, cool sauce

A snack-bar owner carves strips of meat from an enormous piece of skewered lamb.

made from yogurt, garlic, grated cucumbers, olive oil, and mint. The combination of ingredients gives it an interesting flavor that is neither too sour nor too sweet. Its creaminess helps blend with the oiliness of the meat and onions, making every bite simply delightful. Alex, a Greek man and world traveler, explains: "When I tell my old friends who use to live in Greece I am going there, they always ask me to bring them back a souvlaki. . . . The power of souvlaki is strong."[9]

Souvlaki

Souvlaki is not difficult to make. This recipe calls for chunks of lamb. Beef or pork can also be used.

Ingredients:

1 pound lamb, cut into about $\frac{1}{2}$-inch cubes
1 tablespoon olive oil
juice of half a lemon
salt and pepper to taste

Instructions:

1. Combine the olive oil, lemon juice, and salt and pepper.
2. Marinate the meat in the olive-oil mixture for one hour in the refrigerator.
3. Thread the meat onto wood or metal skewers.
4. Grill the meat over an outdoor or indoor grill or in a broiler until it is brown inside and out. If using an indoor grill, use wood skewers that have been soaked in water.
5. Put the meat on plates and serve with tzatziki.

Serves 4

Shopping List
lamb
olive oil
lemon

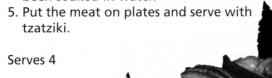

Mezedes

Mezedes are appetizers. Greeks serve them at parties, eat them before meals, and enjoy them as snacks. Popular mezedes include olives bathed in olive oil, fried cheese, tiny triangular pittas stuffed with cheese, meatballs, eggplant paste, sardines rolled in salt, smoked fish, grilled octopus, pickled mushrooms, and fried zucchini.

Syrup Cakes

When Greeks want a sweet snack, they eat syrup cakes. Greeks are known for their sweet tooth, but they never eat pastries after a meal. That, they say, would be too much of a good thing. Instead, they eat fruit after meals, which is better for digestion. That does not mean that Greeks do not eat plenty of pastries. They eat them between meals, before supper, and late at night at *zaharoplasteions*, or pastry shops. Here, Greeks gather at least once a day, drink strong coffee, and eat dozens of sugary treats. In fact, Greeks are so passionate about pastries that the word *zaharoplastis* means "sugar sculpture" in Greek. That is what Greeks believe a well-made pastry is—a work of art.

Among every Greek's favorite works of art are syrup cakes, or sugary yellow cakes bathed in a variety of sweet syrups. So much syrup is used that syrup cakes are eaten with a spoon. That is the way Greeks like all their pastries—the sweeter the better.

This market on Crete is the perfect place to shop for fresh fruit, a favorite Greek dessert.

Syrup cakes are extremely sweet. They are much sweeter than Americans are used to. The cake itself is rich, moist, and spongy. Although most syrup cakes are yellow cakes, they are made with a variety of ingredients. Walnuts, almonds, grated orange rind, yogurt, honey, cinnamon, and cloves are just some of the ingredients used in syrup cakes.

Drenched in Syrup

Syrup cakes are usually baked in long rectangular pans. Once the cake is baked, it is drenched in luscious syrup. To make sure that the syrup reaches the outside and the inside of the cake, bakers use a fork to poke little holes all over the cake. Then they pour on the syrup.

Syrups are made from a number of different ingredients. The flavor and color change depending on the ingredients. Honey, cinnamon-sugar, raisin, lemon, and sour cherry syrups are among the favorites. Orange blossom and rose syrup are two other popular

A priest enjoys a strong cup of coffee with a friend at a pastry shop on the island of Karpathos.

Tzatziki

Tzatziki always accompanies souvlaki. It also makes a great dip on its own. This recipe uses a food processor to grate the cucumbers. The cucumber can be grated by hand and mixed with the other ingredients.

Ingredients:

1 medium cucumber
1 cup plain yogurt
1 tablespoon olive oil
1 teaspoon fresh mint, finely chopped
1 teaspoon garlic powder
salt to taste

Instructions:

1. Wash and peel the cucumber. Cut it into small slices.
2. Put the cucumber slices in the food processor. Add the rest of the ingredients and puree until smooth.
3. Spoon the tzatziki into a bowl, cover, and chill it in the refrigerator for an hour.

Serves 4

Shopping List
cucumber
yogurt
mint
olive oil
garlic powder

flavors. They are made from flower petals and smell as good as they taste.

Greeks make their favorite syrups by combining water, sugar, and other flavors. For example, to make lemon syrup bakers combine water, sugar, and lemon juice. They cook the mixture, stirring constantly, until syrup forms. Once the syrup is ready, it is poured over the cake and left to soak for hours.

Greeks try to match the flavor of the cake to the syrup. They choose flavors that go together well and blend deliciously. Some of their favorite combinations include orange cake with cinnamon syrup, yogurt cake with lemon syrup, almond cake with honey syrup, and walnut cake with honey-lemon syrup. Revani, a rich almond cake with cinnamon-brandy syrup, is probably the most popular of all syrup cakes. After visiting a pastry shop in northern Greece, Kochilas recalls just how popular revani is: "The shop sells nothing but trays and trays of revani . . . for the lines of people who are always waiting, inside and out."[10]

Baklava

Syrup is also an important ingredient in baklava, a flaky pastry that Greeks are wild about. Baklava consists of at least thirty layers of phyllo filled with chopped walnuts, pistachio nuts, almonds, pine nuts, cloves, sugar, and nutmeg.

Baked until it is a golden brown, baklava is topped with a rich syrup made from honey, lemons, oranges, and cinnamon. Cool syrup is used if the pastry is hot, and hot syrup is used if the pastry is cool. Greeks say that more syrup is absorbed this way. To serve, bakers cut the ba-

A baker fills trays of phyllo with nuts, spices, and sugar to make the flaky pastry known as baklava.

klava into diamond-shaped pieces, which Greeks eat at room temperature.

Origins of Baklava

No one knows for sure where baklava originated. Historians say that the first baklava was probably made with bread dough, nuts, and honey by Assyrians in the 8th century B.C. Greek traders brought the recipe back to Greece. Greek cooks, who believed honey and nuts had magical powers, changed the recipe to suit these special foods. Honey, with its bright golden color and incredible sweetness, was thought to be the favorite food of the gods. Nuts were thought to bring good luck to whomever ate them.

Ordinary bread dough was not fitting for such extraordinary foods. So the ancient Greeks used phyllo instead. The results were delectable. Greeks fell in love with the rich sweet treat. That love affair has lasted for centuries. "No other pastry has such a long tradition of pleasing the generations like baklava. Still today, baklava is the number one dessert in Greece,"[11] explains pastry chef Stephen Ordway.

Spoon Sweets

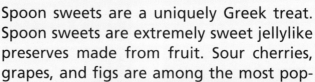

Spoon sweets are a uniquely Greek treat. Spoon sweets are extremely sweet jellylike preserves made from fruit. Sour cherries, grapes, and figs are among the most pop-

ular. Greeks do not spread these preserves on bread or crackers the way Americans do. They eat a spoonful straight from the jar, or they dissolve a spoonful in a glass of cold water and drink it.

Spoon sweets, preserved fruit bits in jelly, are a traditional Greek treat.

A baker on the island of Astipalea displays an assortment of pastries for sale.

A Sweet Good-Bye

Today pastry shops all over Greece sell baklava. It is also often served in Greek homes to visitors before they leave. This is the way Greeks wish their guests a sweet journey.

All over Greece, people are tempted with dozens of wonderful snacks. In homes, sidewalk cafés, street stands, and neighborhood restaurants, the delicious aroma of souvlaki and gyros and the sweet scent of syrup cakes and baklava cast their spell on hungry Greeks.

Special Food with Special Meaning

Greeks love to get together and celebrate. Holidays and important occasions give them an opportunity to gather with loved ones and feast on foods that have special meaning to them.

Christmas Cookies

One way Greeks celebrate the Christmas season is by baking traditional cookies to be shared with family and friends. Spiced honey cookies known as **melomakaronas**, sugar-coated cookies called **kourambiedes**, and **loukoumades**, or fried honey puffs, are found in every Greek home at Christmastime. Vefa Alexiadou, a Greek chef, explains: "All sweet shops decorate their windows with mounds of kourambiedes and melomakaronas. A delectable aroma

A Greek family on the island of Chios enjoys a huge holiday meal together.

A bowl of the syrupy fried treats known as loukoumades is ready to be eaten while a cook prepares a fresh batch.

fills the air of every home kitchen."[12]

Honey and Nuts

Melomakaronas are syrup cookies made of olive oil, orange juice, cinnamon, cloves, and semolina (a type of flour popular in Greece). They are dipped in honey and topped with ground walnuts. Greeks have been eating them since ancient times. Back then, because of their special ingredients—honey and nuts—melomakaronas were eaten only on important occasions. That may be why they have become associated with Christmas.

Loukoumades were another favorite of the ancient Greeks. They too are dipped in honey and covered with walnuts. The ancient Greeks considered loukoumades so precious that they gave them out as prizes at the Olympic games.

Loukoumades are made with yeast, water, and flour. The dough is formed into little balls and fried in olive oil. When the dough hits the hot oil, it puffs up and turns a rich golden brown. While the loukoumades are still hot, bakers pour honey over them and sprinkle them with chopped nuts and cinnamon. At Christmastime, bakers make loukoumades right in the windows of pastry shops throughout Greece, tantalizing holiday shoppers. Vilma Liacouras Chantiles, a Greek chef, explains: "It is fun to see the tiny shops where loukomades are made in the window and where you can stop in for a quick treat."[13]

White Cookies Mean Good Fortune

Kourambiedes are another Christmas favorite. They contain lots of whipped sweet butter, cloves, and almonds. Shaped into little balls, hot kourambiedes are rolled in powdered sugar until they look like tiny snowballs. To Greeks, their whiteness symbolizes purity and happiness. When Greeks eat them at Christmastime, they are wishing each other happiness in the coming year.

Kourambiedes taste of butter, sugar, and almonds. They are both light and rich. "A superlative kourambiede," explains Chantiles, "leaves a

Kourambiedes

These traditional Greek Christmas cookies can be made in many shapes. Balls, ovals, and half-moon shapes are all popular in Greece.

Ingredients:

1 cup unsalted butter, softened
2 cups powdered sugar
1 egg yolk
1 teaspoon vanilla extract
1 teaspoon cinnamon
1 teaspoon ground cloves
2 cups flour
1 cup almonds or walnuts, finely chopped

Shopping List
powdered sugar
eggs
vanilla extract
cinnamon
ground cloves
butter
almonds
flour

Instructions:

1. Preheat the oven to 350 degrees F.
2. Whip the butter and sugar together until the mixture is white and fluffy.
3. Gradually add the egg yolk, vanilla, cinnamon, and cloves and mix well.
4. Gradually add in the flour and mix well. Then add the nuts.
5. Knead the mixture well. The dough should be soft but not crumbly.
6. Grease a cookie sheet.
7. Shape the dough into little balls about the size of a walnut. Place them on the cookie sheet about 3 inches apart.
8. Bake until the cookies are golden, about fifteen minutes.
9. Sprinkle more powdered sugar on the warm cookies. Then allow them to cool before eating.

Makes about 24 cookies

lasting memory—it melts in the mouth and the taster's eyes glow as he rolls the flavor over his tongue, swallows, and sighs ecstatically."[14]

Vassilopitta

New Year's Eve is also celebrated with special foods. For Greeks, New Year's Eve would not be the same without a **vassilopitta**, or St. Vassilios's Bread. This sweet bread is filled with sesame seeds, honey, and oranges.

Vassilopitta is named for St. Basil, the Greek version of Santa Claus. Greek children think he brings them presents on New Year's Day. Like St. Basil's bag, which contains gifts and surprises for Greek children, every vassilopitta contains a surprise—a coin that is baked into the bread. Greek bakers wash the coin and rub it

A tempting display of cookies and pastries is displayed in the window of a bakery located on Ithaca.

A priest in a church on Cyprus blesses loaves of bread as part of an annual religious festival.

with lemon and salt. Then they wrap it in foil and insert it into the dough before the bread is baked. The coin is a symbol of wealth and good fortune.

Finding the Coin

The vassilopitta is served at exactly midnight. The head of the household cuts the bread. Each family member from the oldest to the youngest gets a slice. Everyone hopes that his or her slice has the coin. Whoever gets it, Greeks say, will have good fortune in the coming year.

Everyone has a good time searching for the coin. Alexiadou explains: "One of the few customs which is kept just as alive today as in the past in all Greek homes is the cutting of the vassilopitta. . . . Each one of us

Breads for Every Occasion

Greeks have special breads for every occasion. Sweet breads shaped into rings and decorated with dough flowers are served at weddings. Traditionally, the bride and groom each grab a piece of the ring and pull it apart. It is said that whoever gets the biggest piece will be the boss of the household.

At Christmastime a sweet bread shaped like a cross is often served. The bread is filled with figs, sesame seeds, and oranges and topped with almonds and walnuts. This bread is often decorated with bits of dough that represent the head of the household's profession. For example, little dough fish decorate the bread of a fisherman.

A similar-tasting bread is always served at Easter. This bread is stuffed with red Easter eggs. It is baked with the hard-boiled eggs in it. It can have many shapes. It may be shaped like a fish or a doll, or it may be long and braided.

Another sweet bread is made in the summer to celebrate the birthday of St. Fanourios. Greek folklore says that if a young girl puts a piece of this walnut-filled bread under her pillow, she will see the face of her future husband in her dreams.

These breads shaped like crosses, rings, and other symbols will be served at a wedding celebration.

A shepherd on the island of Levkas drives his sheep to market. Lamb is a traditional Easter dish in Greece.

believes in the good fortune that the coin will bring if it happens to be in our slice."[15] No matter who gets the coin, vassilopitta is so sweet, soft, and luscious that everyone is happy when it is served.

Easter Lamb

Easter is another holiday marked by special foods. Most Greeks are religious people. Because of their religious beliefs, they often give up many of their favorite foods during Lent, the forty-day period before Easter. When Easter arrives, they are ready to feast.

Roast lamb is usually the centerpiece of the Easter feast. Eating lamb at Easter, Greeks say, represents their love of Jesus Christ, who is frequently called "the Lamb of God." In the days before Easter, outdoor markets throughout Greece offer shoppers recently slaughtered lambs that have been skinned and gutted and are ready to cook. Greeks crowd these markets, making their Easter purchase. A traveler recalls: "We found a parking lot full of refrigerated trucks, each with a crowd at the back and one or two men inside the truck bringing out lambs. . . . As Easter Sunday came closer and closer, more and more people walked the streets of downtown Athens carrying their lambs."[16]

Most Greeks slowly spit roast the whole lamb outdoors over an open fire. To flavor the lamb, cooks rub it inside and out with olive oil and lemon. They also rub the spit with lemon, then pass it through the lamb, whose legs have been tied together. Then they place the spit between two forked ends of iron poles that are inserted into the ground near the fire.

To ensure that the lamb cooks evenly, the spit must be turned. In the past, different family members would take turns cranking a handle on the end of the spit to turn it. Today the spit turns mechanically, which is good, because a 10-pound (5kg) lamb takes about four hours to cook. Cooks still must brush the lamb with olive oil and lemon juice as it cooks to keep it from drying out.

Easter Roasted Potatoes

Roasted potatoes usually are served with lamb at Easter. These are easy to make. The recipe calls for peeled potatoes, but clean unpeeled potatoes work well too.

Shopping List
potatoes
olive oil
lemon juice

Ingredients:

2 pounds red potatoes
1/2 cup extra-virgin olive oil
1/2 cup fresh lemon juice
1 teaspoon salt
1/2 teaspoon black pepper

Instructions:

1. Preheat oven to 450 degrees F.
2. Wash and peel the potatoes. Cut them into bite-size chunks.
3. Combine olive oil, lemon juice, and salt and pepper in a large plastic bag.
4. Put potato chunks in the bag, seal the bag, and shake until the potatoes are coated with the olive oil mixture.
5. Place potatoes in a single layer in a baking dish or on a baking sheet.
6. Bake for about forty minutes. Turn the potatoes over after twenty minutes. The potatoes are done when they are soft and golden brown.

Serves 4

Spits of lamb roast over an enormous open fire in the mountains of Crete. Greeks have prepared lamb this way for eons.

When the lamb is ready, the outside is crisp and brown. The meat is so tender that it can be easily pulled off the bone. Before it is served, the lamb is removed from the spit and carved into slices. Easter lamb is usually served with roasted potatoes, fresh bread, olives, spanakopitta, and salad.

An Ancient Practice

Even before Greeks started celebrating Easter, they commonly ate lamb in the spring. Baby lambs are born in the spring, and the younger the animal the more tender the meat. The ancient Greeks always served them at their spring festivals. They cooked them in much the same way

Diples Double the Wealth

On New Year's Day, at weddings, and at baptisms, diples are always served. Diples are light, air-filled pastries topped with honey and cinnamon. Deep-fried in olive oil, a diple may be flat and wide resembling a little dough wallet, shaped into a bow, or twirled and braided into a long coil.

Because the word *diple* means "double" in Greek, Greeks say that eating the fried pastry on New Year's Day doubles a person's good luck and wealth in the coming year. Eating diples at a wedding, doubles the bride and groom's happiness. Eating diples at a baptism, Greeks say, doubles the new baby's life span.

as modern Greeks do. Archaeologists have found ancient spit-roasting equipment and lamb bones throughout Greece. Feasting on spit-roasted lamb in the spring was so common among ancient Greeks that the writer Homer mentioned it in his writing. For modern Greeks, it would not be Easter without roasted lamb. Chef Peter Conistis explains: "In Greece with spring comes Easter, and with Easter comes lamb."[17]

Whether it is spit-roasted lamb for Easter, vassilopitta on New Year's Eve, or melomakaronas, kourambiedes, and loukoumades at Christmastime, food plays an important role in Greek life. Special foods with special meanings make Greek holiday celebrations memorable. Without them, Greek holidays would not be so unique or so much fun.

Metric Conversions

Mass (weight)

1 ounce (oz.)	= 28.0 grams (g)
8 ounces	= 227.0 grams
1 pound (lb.) or 16 ounces	= 0.45 kilograms (kg)
2.2 pounds	= 1.0 kilogram

Liquid Volume

1 teaspoon (tsp.)	= 5.0 milliliters (ml)
1 tablespoon (tbsp.)	= 15.0 milliliters
1 fluid ounce (oz.)	= 30.0 milliliters
1 cup (c.)	= 240 milliliters
1 pint (pt.)	= 480 milliliters
1 quart (qt.)	= 0.95 liters (l)
1 gallon (gal.)	= 3.80 liters

Pan Sizes

8-inch cake pan	= 20 x 4-centimeter cake pan
9-inch cake pan	= 23 x 3.5-centimeter cake pan
11 x 7-inch baking pan	= 28 x 18-centimeter baking pan
13 x 9-inch baking pan	= 32.5 x 23-centimeter baking pan
9 x 5-inch loaf pan	= 23 x 13-centimeter loaf pan
2-quart casserole	= 2-liter casserole

Length

1/4 inch (in.)	= 0.6 centimeters (cm)
1/2 inch	= 1.25 centimeters
1 inch	= 2.5 centimeters

Temperature

212° F	= 100° C (boiling point of water)
225° F	= 110° C
250° F	= 120° C
275° F	= 135° C
300° F	= 150° C
325° F	= 160° C
350° F	= 180° C
375° F	= 190° C
400° F	= 200° C

Chapter 1: The Unique Flavors of Greek Cooking

1. Aglaia Kremezi, *The Foods of Greece*. New York: Stewart, Tabori & Chang, 1993, p. 17.
2. Quoted in Diane Kochilas, *The Food and Wine of Greece*. New York: St. Martin's Press, 1990, p. 13.
3. Kochilas, *The Food and Wine of Greece,* p. 23.

Chapter 2: Favorite Foods

4. Kremezi, *The Foods of Greece,* p. 205.
5. Kochilas, *The Food and Wine of Greece,* p. 111.
6. Quoted in Diane Kochilas, *The Glorious Foods of Greece*. New York: William Morrow, 2001, p. 367.
7. Alexandra Tsakiridou, "Moussaka—a Traditional Greek Recipe," http://pierna.spark.net.gr/etimes/moussaka.htm.
8. Spetses Direct, "Horiatiki—Greek Salad," www.spetsesdirect.com/atasteofspetses/GreekSalad/horiatiki.htm.

Chapter 3: Snacks and Sweets

9. Alex Charalabidis, "Souvlaki: The Hamburger of Greece," Greek Foods, www.greekfoods.com/souvlaki.html.

10. Kochilas, *The Food and Wine of Greece*, p. 302.
11. Stephen Ordway, "About Our Baklava," the Best Baklava, www.the-best-baklava.com/aboutourbaklava.html.

Chapter 4: Special Food with Special Meaning

12. Vefa Alexiadou, "Cuisine and Greek Tradition," Vefa's House, www.add.gr/comp/vefa/grcuis.htm.
13. Vilma Liacouras Chantiles, *The Food of Greece*. New York: Fireside, 1975, p. 274.
14. Chantiles, *The Food of Greece*, p. 314.
15. Alexiadou, "Cuisine and Greek Tradition."
16. Greek Foods, "Naxos Easter Lamb and Cheese Market," www.greekfoods.com/naxosmarket/index.html.
17. Peter Conistis, *Greek Cuisine: The New Classics*. Berkeley, CA: Ten Speed Press, 1994, p. 87.

avgolemono: A popular Greek sauce made by combining lemon juice, egg yolks, and chicken broth.

bechamel: A white sauce that is put on top of moussaka.

cured: To preserve a food by treating it with a salt solution.

dolmades: Stuffed grape leaves.

extra-virgin olive oil: The oil extracted the first time olives are pressed.

gyros: Sandwiches made with grilled meat.

horiatiki: A popular Greek salad made with tomatoes, onions, olives, and feta cheese.

kourambiedes: Greek butter cookies served at Christmastime.

ladolemono: A sauce made from olive oil and lemons.

loukoumades: Fried honey puffs.

melomakaronas: Honey cookies popular at Christmastime.

moussaka: A casserole made with layers of eggplant, potatoes, onions, red peppers, and lamb.

phyllo: A paper-thin pastry dough.

pittas: The Greek word for pies.

rotisserie: A skewer that turns over a heat source. Meat is cooked on it.

souvlaki: Meat cooked on a skewer and served with onions and tomatoes.

tzatziki: A sauce made from yogurt, garlic, cucumber, olive oil, and mint.

vassilopitta: A sweet bread that has a coin baked into it and is served on New Year's Eve.

zaharoplasteions: Pastry shops.

For Further Exploration

Books

Arlette N. Braman, *Kids Around the World Cook! The Best Food and Recipes from Many Lands.* Hoboken, NJ: John Wiley, 2000. This book contains recipes from many countries including Greece.

Laurie Carlson, *Classical Kids: An Activity Guide to Life in Ancient Greece and Rome.* Chicago: Chicago Review, 1998. Discusses life in ancient Greece, including foods, with many activities.

Meredith Costain, *Welcome to Greece.* Langhorne, PA: Chelsea House, 2001. A simple book filled with photos and facts about Greece, including a recipe.

Marcia S. Gresko, *Letters Home from Greece.* Woodbridge, CT: Blackbirch, 1999. Information about Greek people, daily life, food, and land presented through letters from a young traveler.

Matthew Locricchio, *Cooking of Greece.* New York: Benchmark, 2004. A Greek recipe book for teenagers.

Lynne W. Villios, *Cooking the Greek Way: Revised and Expanded to Include New Low-Fat and Vegetarian Recipes.* Minneapolis: Lerner, 2001. A Greek cookbook for kids.

Web Sites

Eat Greek Tonight (www.eatgreektonight.com). This site offers lots of Greek recipes.

Go Greece (www.gogreece.com/cuisine/cookbook). This site has lots of Greek recipes.

Greek Foods (www.greekfoods.com). A guide to Greek food with recipes, pictures of Greek dishes, and information about how food is served in Greek homes and restaurants.

Greece for Girl Scouts (http://coy.ne.client2.attbi. com/Greece-GS.html). A great site with links to information about Greek food, music, clothes, geography, history, culture, language, famous people, and more.

Think Quest (www.thinkquest.org/library/search.html). This site provides thirty-four links to information about ancient Greece, the Olympics, Greek dance, famous Greeks, and Greek culture.

Index

Picture Credits

About the Author

Barbara Sheen has been an author and educator for more than thirty years. Her writing has been published in the United States and in Europe. She writes in both English and Spanish. She lives in New Mexico with her family. In her spare time, she likes to swim, walk, bike, garden, and cook.